Trout Stream Creed

Trout Stream Creed

David Carpenter

COTEAU BOOKS
WWW.COTEAUBOOKS.COM

Edited by Don McKay.
Cover and book design by Duncan Campbell.
Cover photo, "Trout in a Pool at Seven Falls," © Lake County Museum/CORBIS/MAGMA.
Author photo by Dark Horse Studio, Saskatoon.
Printed and bound in Canada at Houghton Boston Lithographers, Saskatoon.

National Library of Canada Cataloguing in Publication

Carpenter, David, 1941-
Trout stream creed / David Carpenter.

Poems.
ISBN 1-55050-266-2

I. Title.
PS8555.A76158T76 2003   C811'.54   C2003-911141-5

1   2   3   4   5   6   7   8   9   10

Available in the US and Canada from:
Fitzhenry & Whiteside
401-2206 Dewdney Ave.   195 Allstate Parkway
Regina, Saskatchewan   Markham, Ontario
Canada   S4R 1H3   Canada   L3R 4T8

The publisher gratefully acknowledges the financial assistance of the Saskatchewan Arts Board, the Canada Council for the Arts, the Government of Canada through the Book Publishing Industry Development Program (BPIDP), the Government of Saskatchewan, through the Cultural Industries Development Fund, and the City of Regina Arts Commission, for its publishing program.

This book is for Kever

Table of Contents

Rediscovery of a Poem I Wrote a Long Time Ago

I

A battalion of tractor mowers
is swarming over the golf course today
each one but mine droning droning droning
in ever decreasing circles
around the oaks and appletrees.
My mower's out of whack again and
again I am singled out by my boss.
Ask Manpower for groundsmen, yass?
They sand-it nutcases and flowerheads.
I wonder which kind of bumbler I am.

Gloss 1

Tractor mowers he can handle. He shouldn't have to deal with me. I know this now. Forty years ago I'm a lounger, a burgeoning poet. I read poetry alone in the darkest corners of certain bars. I write poetry in the Java Shop on Jasper Avenue. I do these things so people will notice, and I am not bothered by the fact that the golf course in my poem is full of appletrees. On the job I'm a fuckup, a layabout, okay? There, I've admitted it. A fuck-up and middle class to boot. But back then I am sensitive. I'm a nice guy. I feel sorry for people less fortunate than me. The children in Dickens's novels, for example.

2

In June the best shade for loungers
is under the flowering crab.
Breathing the breath of blossoms
I forget the man I work for.
I forget all the men I've ever known
who are dumb dumb dumb
dumb to the hum above me
        the only sound now
        the mantra of thousands of bumblebees.

Gloss 2

The mantra of thousands of bumblebees. I'll bet I congratulated myself on this line, how it testified to all that was knowing and cosmic about me. The man I work for is Dennis. He hates all Russians, the Soviet Union, all communists, sees them everywhere. Dennis is from a farm in Northern Alberta that went belly up. He came to the city with a grade five education. His family is from what we used to call the Ukraine. There too the farm went belly up. *Avry year,* Dennis tells me, *I work like shit, nodding to show for.* Sometimes he looks at me as though he understands the reason for the Bolshevik Revolution.

3

My silences are as
suspect as the bees
come to sting him
things to fear.
Yet they are here
not for stinging but
with pollenheavy legs
to fumble and sing round the blossoms
     a thing I cannot tell him.

Gloss 3

I work here so that I can go to university in the fall. Dennis is working here so that he can raise a family and live like people in the city. We are both working here so that people with leisure can come and play golf. I asked Dennis once if he ever golfed and he looked like he wanted to swat me. Later he asked me if I was ever going to golf here, at this course, and I said I didn't know how. For a while that day Dennis picked on someone else.

4

It would be
clever of me
to find some meaning
in this moment.
A long line of sweat runs down the backbone of my brain.
Nothing.
So I think of nothing until
with a wrench
my boss has fixed the mower.

Gloss 4

I still like this stanza. Maybe I wasn't a complete imbecile.

And then it comes to me
all that I cannot tell him
a prayer for nutcases and flowerheads to mumble
on the seats of tractor mowers:
> *Appletree for the sake of honey*
> *For this lying prone*
> *beneath your storm of petals*
> *I am become your drone*
> *not dumb but one*
> *with the humming moment.*
> *For the sake of apples*
> *bid me unthink me*

Gloss 5

Bid me unthink me? I used to know what that meant. Bid me unthink me. You had to be young and prone to be that deep.

Like the kids next door. All they do is party. Every weekend these parties begin at midnight and they play rock n roll till six in the morning. Their own music on their own instruments with speakers the size of shithouses. Their music is white rock n roll, rich white kids' rock n roll.
One of them says he's a poet. He's just as obnoxious as his friends. The kids next door are all learning how to drink, how to barf into the neighbours' flowerbeds. My wife and I don't get a lot of sleep on weekends. I confront these brats all the time. They look right through me. Flowerheads and nutcases.

Bid me unthink me.

And I know what's going on here. It's sex. They call it sexuality now but it's sex, that's the key to it. Hormones coursing like cheap wine through their veins.

5 (continued)

For the sake of apples
bid me unthink me
bid me like bees
ease into the nectar
or like nodding blossoms
give tongue to the bees.

Gloss 5 (continued)

That's it, the poem Dennis inspired. I never saw him again. I don't miss him, but I'd like the chance to talk with him now.

I don't miss the boy I was. I don't miss the stupidity, the uncertainties of romance, the conviction that this weekend I'm gonna get lucky. Or being a lounger and a fuckup on the job. I don't miss that magical capacity to exclude all middleaged or boring people from my range of vision. I don't miss being a moral imbecile, distanced from anything that matters. I don't miss the semen factory I used to carry like a dumb friend between my legs. I don't miss my lean body, my innocent smile, my hair, my insouciant charm, my girlfriends.

> But sometimes I miss the unthink me, the path
> going over and back from the hairy legs of the bees
> to the beckoning flowers.
> I don't miss the places where I lounged
> among the acorn casings blossoms books
> and fancies under the appletree
> I don't even miss the honey.
> I miss what the honey meant to me.

(1964-2001)

A Wedding

And do you take this man
he asks
and awaits her reply almost
it would seem
with regret.
His manner is reserved
but his eyes keep returning to her
to the flowing swells and slendernesses.
Do they trace those veiled contours
the tresses, the suggestion of her breasts?
I think so.
For his pale blue eyes seek a chastened refuge on me
and dwell rather too briefly on her.

Her whose hair will tumble down her back tonight
dismissing this chaste event.
I have seen this beauty many times before
her beauty
which is pain for him.
I see it now
framed and sanctified
in plastic rimmed mirrors.

I see it now like islands
on the globes of his eyes
which blink and dart occasionally
on scriptures old with words.

(1968)

Garden Spider

her most insidious designs
bright and euclidean
each filament
sagging with dew
like strands of pearls

at night the hunting is best
a hapless moth flutters out
strikes the web
      the great dancer
      gathers it into her embrace
      in a last paralytic second
      the frantic and impassioned moth
      receives the kiss
      of her devoured suitors

when her own time comes
she clenches her legs
gathers them in as if to hide
in her own crabbed and furry hermitage

as she shrinks into a diminishing ball
one set of eyes still scanning the web
she glimpses a last monstrous imago
growing huge with its approach
the dancing rhythms the scuttle the
tarantulations of her maker

(1976)

Pen-elopings

how easily you dance

           between

                      my

    words

flirting with them
leaping

           through them
without getting   singed
but they never intercept you
you make them

        jump the ship
they try to   anchor you
but how to   anchor you
who ought to   anchor me
while I circle you with words:

how serenely you read by the bedside lamp
I say
o moonlike watchful anchoress
I say
you are in love
there are two kinds of women
the one to voyage out for
the one to return to
when voyages are done
you are the second kind

what worries me is
I come home
to find you
gone on a voyage

(1977)

Porcelain

it's more delicate than most clay
that's why I work in porcelain
she tells me
tanned feet, faded

violet house dress
flecked with porcelain
violet flarings
in her eyes

here, she says, I'll show you
hikes up her dress
and it's not just the feet that are tanned
she straddles

the wheel like a cellist
I straddle a chair
our knees face one another
she wets the centred wedge, kicks

the wheel into a spin
I watch the motion of her leg
turn the wet mound in her hands
she holds it like a bouquet

it flowers up between her hands
a pestle for a mortar, she says
runs her fingers lightly
up the blooming pillar

I could have said something
but what do you say
when someone is spinning you
spinning you around

my soul is blooming like that mound
I could have said that without lying
have mercy
I could have said that

but she was someone's lover
so I bought four cups and left
this happened a long time ago
the last cup cracked this morning

I am putting this down
as much as I remember
to throw her likeness
        something doomed

doomed and perfect
but most of all
I think
because all her cups are gone

(1978)

Mrs. Ratzlaff's Recipe for Drought

Take a musty shroud for oak antiques and call it her sweater
take a faded thin old curtain and call it her dress
hang them on a shrivelled bony thing
with prune lips puckered in a permanent grin
the grin of a dying rat will do
take and crumple brown paper bags
and call them the skin on her face neck hands
take a sickle and call it her spine
and you have the husk that holds
the blooming dreams of Mrs. Ratzlaff
who says she's older than Elijah

the hose she is holding sways slowly back and forth
take a long green snake rising fom wet coils
a snake she may have charmed ages ago
and call it her hose

cycling by you stop for a moment
hi you say   hoping not to sound young whatcha doing
in a voice old as Elijah she says
flowers gut to heff vater too
you betcha my life

she stands with the hose motionless on the lawn
take a burr oak and call it her stillness
the stillness of tulips and the appletrees and roses
that she waters in the gritty spring air
steeped in the off-yellows
and the dust that puffs up everywhere
but in her yard

in her soil the moist bulbs of daffodils
will burst with jonquil insomnia
among the uncurling ferns
and she will be there suckling the flora
when the sky turns to dirty violet
and sinks into the purple of rotting plums
her flowerbeds are loamblack damp and musky
with earthworms twining
take the pink veins of your body
and as she shrivels
call them her worms

she is stingy with her water
the hose has learned where to spray
and six inches into Mrs. Varga's yard
would be rank promiscuity
so Mrs. Varga's grass is dry beige and brittle
more faded than the tatters on Mrs. Ratzlaff's head
but her own grass is green

she stands on the lawn
she may be standing here
when we've finished this poem
the arms extend from the sickle spine
the passionate grip
her hands on the hose
is a sign I think
to fickle time
in an hour when bushes burn
and green things are dying

(1979)

the poet's eye

writing I
always turn my back
to the ocean
convinced that's when
the orcas come

    bursting from their pod
    rolling in a fine frenzy
    they are like nothing else
    megadolphin
    ultrasalmon
    the orcas breach
    pause in the air for photos
    re-enter sirensinging in orcasian
    each breach and re-entry
    a tidal wave
    a wave hello
    a detonation
    a party I'm not
    invited to a ballet
    of under
    statement a

finished for the day I
turn around and look at the ocean
(that neptuningforktongued mother of us all)
and they're gone

(1980)

Urban Eschatology

the nine-year-old girl
who claims she loves everything
the one with the dimple
brown shoulderlength hair

is missing
there is talk
of a middleaged man in the park
no one knows for sure

it's been eight days now
we see her photo everywhere
she seems to be everywhere
you know   rumours

garbage collectors have been
asked to rip open the glad bags
we can see her curled up
in so many

those with hindsight say
we should have started ripping them open
the day she disappeared
she's out there in the dump under everything

everything conspires against her
being found
anything could conceal her
she's not very big

we see her in wrecked cars fridges
ditches back alleys public dumps
plastic bags garbage cans
shallow graves everything

she'll turn up say a few optimists
the least hopeful among us
use the same words
she'll turn up

eyes beholding the last things
the way the man smiled
saw that she was fair
claimed her for his own

(1983)

The Poem for My Mother

might never get written.
If it were it would be wholesome
have none of those words we use
when we've run out of nice ones
something she could show her friends.
My poem would have none of the current gloom
(You always write such gloomy things)
it might have romance but no sex
I'd take the advice from the woman in South Pacific
Happy talk, keep talkin happy talk.
This would be a good exercise for me
I'd go back to basics
grass mountains sunlight a bird or two
perhaps a plane overhead
(it couldn't be a combat plane or a bomber
or anything commercial that could get hijacked
or one of those jumbo jets that
okay forget the plane)
Like I say I'd return to basics
the jewel in the Ethiop's ear
but no starving Ethiopians.

I'll let you in on a little secret.
I showed Mum the first part of this thing.
I'd been thinking it might even be finished
but she was not impressed.
It's not you I'm writing about   I said.
What do you mean   she said
you've only got one mother.
And what's this guff about romance but no sex?
She showed me a book she'd been reading.
Holy cow, I said.

You see my problem here?
I've been writing a poem
for a mother I've given birth to
who's nothing like my mum
or at least not enough like Mum
to be my mother.
I suppose I could tell her
how to comport herself at her age
suggest some dear-sweet-little-old-lady books
but she'd just give me a look
and go back to being her.

Anyway   this poem
I'm still going to write it.
Perhaps I'll wait till she's a little older
or the headlines are a bit more cheerful.
I want my poem to soar with words
like hope loyalty honour goodness love peace
passion too   why not
words that wait like whitehaired ladies
for their sons to take them home.
We'll see if I'm up to it.
She tells me she's not holding her breath.

(1986)

The Trout Stream Creed

At this moment, Dear Readers, neither you nor I
    stand hip-deep in a trout stream.
    This fact distresses me.
    It undermines my rhetoric.
    So wade in, look upstream, always upstream.
    That's very important.
    The feeding trout also look upstream
    waiting for supper.
    You can sneak up on them.
    The stream flows all around your body.
    It welcomes you by cooling your body.
    Even if you are not naturally inclined to panegyrics
    your body will be.
    It will thank you for entering the stream on such a hot day.
    It will sing songs of praise
    for the flowing world you have entered.
    Your body already believes in trout streams
            their gravelly bottoms
            their secret murmurs
            their noonday effulgence
            the purity of their water
            their green pools and silver riffles

the way they embrace a big boulder
the overhanging trees that bend to them
    as priests to the virgin
the trout that haunt them like so many
    semen in the birth canal
brook trout brown trout cutthroat rainbow.

In a trout stream I can feel the supreme inviolability
    at the heart of all creation.
    Critics beware: this is not meant casually
    and above all not ironically, okay?
    This is a religious utterance, do I make myself clear?
    Don't mess with this one.

Once out of a trout stream I believe in the virus
    at the heart of all creation.
    Adam had herpes even before Eve.
    He was a herpetologist.
    He got it from the snake.

I believe for every drop of rain that falls
    an acid lurks.

Do I contradict myself?
 Did Walt Whitman?
 Is the Pope Catholic?

A belief is a leaf that wants to be.
 The Pope believes in God.
 Whitman believes in leaves.
 Therefore (Fill in the blanks. Five points for a good syllogism, ten
 points if it flows nicely, fifteen if it's got some trout in it. The trout
 have to be alive. Remember, we're in this thing together. I
 don't know about you, but my waders are leaking.)

I believe that in the first sip of coffee at 7:00 a.m.
 the first tug of draft
 that last shrimp on the serving plate at the Saigon Rose
 there is a local divinity
 a little spirit who knows what you like
 an alfred e. numinous little godling.
 He is everywhere I have been.
 When I was a boy he used to cling
 to the cashews in the bowl of mixed nuts.

I believe I have said too much.
    I believe I have meant too little.

When brought before his maker
    the German says *Ich glaube an Gott*
    the Frenchman says *Je crois en Dieu*
    the Englishman says *I believe in God, yes quite*
    the American says *I believe in America*
    the Japanese investment banker says *I too believe in America*
    the Canadian says *that depends, eh?*

At me the buck stops, the bucks turn to leaves, the leaves turn in your
fingers, and if you've come this far, your waders are leaking too.
Upstream. Let us go upstream from whence cometh our salvation.

Another test to wade through. This too is about fundamental belief.
When a hungry tribe of Tyrannosaurus Rexes descends on
Broadway Avenue, and one of them reaches with its scaly forefoot for
your vitals do you

a) dial 911
b) wonder if your policy covers dinosaur attacks
c) grab for your shotgun
d) grab for your vitals
e) pray?

If you grab for your vitals
    perhaps like me
    you believe in vitality.

About a century ago, a Cree chief named Thunderchild told a Métis guide named Pete Lafleur of a stream flowing west out of the foothills of Central Alberta that came to be known as Alford Creek. The old chief told this guide that as long as this stream ran clear and sweet, there would be trout for everyone, and *everything,* he said, *would be fine.* When Pete Lafleur was an old man, he told my Grandfather Carpenter, whose survey crew he was guiding through the Alford Creek country. My grandfather told my father, who told my brother, who told me. (The next day I went fishing.) And as you and I drift into the ocean on a wave of chemicals, offal, and comfortable assertions, I am telling you, the old chief was right.

If I wrote the Prime Minister, and informed him that trout streams are the fallopian tubes of the nation, do you think he would believe me? Well, they are, Sir. The trout in these waters are a synecdoche for happy times. They are the answer to your prayers, Mr. Prime Minister. And hey, let's get the Y out of your. Let's get into this thing together. I know, Sir. Our waders are leaking. But remember, the small miracle that just swam between your legs has been speaking with the chief.

Dear Waders,

Have you ever looked at a spawning brook trout?
Have you ever seen
the back and the top of the head
(those olive green vermiculations)
the sides
(those discrete red spots surrounded by bluish halos)
the lower belly
(those bright orange flanks)
the fins
(those black and red flickers with creamy edges)
the dorsal fin
(those wavy lines, that marbled look)
the imprints on your retina when they come up for a fly
(those flashes of iridescence)?

I don't know what happened to the brook trout in Alford Creek. Perhaps an honest realtor from the nearby town can tell you. So maybe you think this thing I wrote is an elegy. Well, it's not. I'd rather you read it the way you read the water during a mayfly hatch. I'd rather you read it as a bit of practical advice from a how-to book or a recipe. I'd rather you read it as a love letter from someone believed missing or long dead, a carping old geezer who stalks your dreams by night, who stocks your streams by day.

I believe in the primacy, the utter importance, of trout streams.
    I believe they come from God.
    I'm not sure about God
    but I'm sure about trout streams.

I believe in every 2nd thing on Broadway Avenue (that's in Saskatoon):
    the Cheese Shop
    the Broadway Café
    a restaurant called Calories
    the OK Economy
    the gal behind the till in the OK Economy
    I think her name is Alma
    she has a nice smile
    the Broadway Theatre
    a blues bar named Bud's
    Lydia's, a smoky refuge for tortured genius
    the Four-Corner Bookstore
    the Broadway Shoe Repair
    Mr. Willey's Watch Repair
    the Roastery
    Amigo's
    those places that proclaim that they are here to stay.

There's an allnight restaurant in San Antonio called Earl
            Able's. It has sixty-year-old waitresses with beehive
            hairdos as blonde and unapologetic as corn niblets.
            I believe in that too.

I believe in God sometimes.
            About as often, I suspect, God believes in me.

I believe in lovemaking at any time of the morning
Vivaldi in the hands of the young
hot caramel fudge sundaes
unlimited sexual freedom for all
species of wildlife
except mosquitoes

(and sometimes in the afternoon too).

(1991)

up here spring is

all sand and dung and grit in your teeth and
the smudgy wind sends down the gulls
to flock to the garbage dump and
Jennys and Shelleys walk in their wellies
up and down the lanes looking for loonies
hey, what's that   'sa nother condom
what are they for   never mind says Shelley
no that's not a loonie that's a bottlecap and
all you know is a condom is for sure a filthy thing
and a tampon is to stamp on splash
like that.

When all is sand and dung and
God how many colours can bubblegum be
green now purple now day-glo pink
the backagain crows are calling
down from the smudgepot sky to the melting muck and
the ice is black as blackbirds pecking on the gravelscabbed snow
O it's spring has come on winter's fur behind
and meeyowls in the bubblegum lanes all night
and the sandblaster wind is enough
to keep the balloonman at home all day
to miss the muddy glory from the spinning wheels
of the bus on Route 6a.

How the sidestreets swell and flow like
the nostrils of the common cold and
the melting dirt smells like the first day
you ever catch a line drive
you are filthy heroes
mucking to the majors
smell the spores of
winter's dung the grass is
brownish grey
unriz on the grimy snow
so off you go into the sandblaster wind
and the gulls yammer over the bottlecap lanes
no that's not a loonie
that's a moray mouth agape for life to rise and burst
like a broken water main.

And down the lane you go and
Jenny's mother says to her little brother
did you put that in your mouth
spit it out   you spit that out. Thank you. Yuk.
And past Jenny's yard the melted snow eels deep into the ice
so all night long the gutters will sing chthonic
to the cats in the tampon lanes and
you dream you are with Shelley and her sisters
(those girls down the street who can find a lover in a plover)
look there now
she is bending to pick to grab to grasp....

But just as you are rising like the long-gone sun and
fear you may never get back to Shelley and
the thing she grasps with her wonderful fingers
in the pulsing place where you know who you are
your mother   your mother   your mother
                        is calling your name.

(1993)

February

In my dream I ask you when will winter end and you say when hope begins and I say when and you say whenever and I say how do you hope and you say hang out hope and I say how and you say hang out hope like a cantilever and I wake up and remember you are somewhere in Tennessee.

On a windy February night alone in the house with your beloved gone to Graceland you don't want to catch yourself waiting for spring. It might well be spring in Graceland but you're closer to Iceland than Graceland. Don't talk to me of spring. Just let the winter be over. That will do just fine.

The snow has an icy carapace as hard as frozen bark the streets are rutted with ruts as hard as rails the ice is forever like death and taxes and hope has left the building and you've figured out why the ice is forever it's because in February it's always February.

The wind the wind the snowless wind the glazing wind it can't wait to get down to North Dakota for some cross-border shopping it smells like perpetual motion it smells like the track suit of a marathon runner with insomnia it smells of all the little nullities we have gathered since November it smells of waiting and waiting on a windy night until you come home to me with a March an April bloom on your face or some evidence of returning life and you say did anyone call and all I can say is February. February. I can only pronounce this word correctly in the summertime when my lips aren't so numb and when I say February it gives my lips an aerobic workout like chewing on raw rhubarb.

All night long the sky over Saskatoon is an orange halo surrounded by all the darkness in the universe an orange as elusive as Elvis and I dream of gardens in Victoria and those tweedy voices on the tv garden shows the ones who spot an early budding rose and say *oh what have we here* and I wake up three four times because you are not here and in my dream I am always waiting for winter to end.

Melt is a word in someone else's lexicon all over the yard and down the lane and out across the prairie snow is a glazed expanse for the wind to sail past the snow wants to be ice but it can't the ice wants to be snow to lie as elegant as snow should lie it only wants to be what it can never be and so do I so I lean out hope like a cantilever less for the cant and more for the lever the heart says soon the wind says never.

(1994)

Nipawin Hospital, September 6, 1995

for Kever

All night long wrapped in a bedsheet
she sat by my cot
spooning icecubes into my mouth.
Once in a while she bowed down her head
to snatch a moment of sleep.

Not once did I move or dare
to move one inch in my cot
waiting for my blood
(what she called my stubborn blood)
to clot.

The room was cold
the sheet was white.
That's the key to the whole thing.
The way it covered her head
and body, the way it lay
like snow in the night—
reminded me of Muslim women.

And this is the picture of love I keep
this year's favourite centrefold
cloaked in a sheet
to keep out the cold.

(1995)

Beating the Clock

Each morning the alarm sears through my chest
Abuzz with its convulsive mortal tone;
I learn once more the thing I've always known:
That death some day will choose to love me best.
I'm just awake; it scuttles up to me,
A hesitation lurking in my breath,
A ticking premonition of my death—
How dry as cobs and puckered fruit I'll be.
And nothing much around to say that I
Was here and loved and laughed like any guy.
So, here's my work and here's my play.
It rests upon a library shelf.
Now death can suck my breath away
Then death can go and fuck itself.

(1997)

My Father's Dying

blocked arteries from a massive heart attack
alzheimer's aphasia dementia three kinds of cancer
Death is confused
Death wants a second opinion

Dad the father   Dad the son   Dad the
family tyrant with a short fuse   a ready laugh
ready laugh and a short fuse
awakens every morning with clenched fists
like a man in a brawl
around him don't let your guard down
above all   never admit to a weakness
if it hurts don't let it show

they'll skin you alive
they'll cut you in two
they were the government
the rival team   rival companies
cars on a busy road   your boss   senior colleagues
the banks   all other loaning agencies   society
never let your guard down

on the subject of various girls
don't get involved
politics
don't get involved
idealistic causes
don't get involved
learning to play an instrument
don't get involved
learning to save money
now yer talkin

a big kid known as Shags
used to swagger down into the ravine
and beat the crap out of us
I told him once if he tried that again
my dad would come to his home
and kick him in the nuts
for some reason the kid never tried it again
which made me wonder about the magic of words
and the omnipotence of my father

he could have died in World War II
but they sent him packing
tuberculosis they said   blood in the urine
thirty-five years old and a kid in the cradle
they sent him back to Edmonton
one in the cradle another on the way
the writer of these lines
his scornful son

the coronary came at sixty-three
Mum phoned me from the hospital
I spotted her standing outside the ward
as soon as she saw me she shook her head
no   her gesture said
he's not going to make it
thirty-one years ago

when your father is over ninety
senile and dying
however slowly
you tend to seek advice
doctors lawyers social workers
counsellors health professionals
they all say the same thing
take his car away

he should have died in World War II
but they sent him packing
lungs a-hacking
the rest won't rhyme

my father gets smaller and smaller by the year
smaller by the month
cancer in the lymphatic system
cancer in the prostate
cancers all over his head
seep and bleed and fester anew
like a bombed-out town
like World War II
the rest won't rhyme
I play on my harp from time to time
the rest won't rhyme

good to see you Dad
how'd you get out here
took the plane   how are you feeling
your mother's ready to go dancing
good for her
how'd you get out here
I took the plane
you take the car this time

he used to drive downtown and get lost
try to go home to the old house
with the new owners
his license had been suspended
his insurance invalid
I took the bull by the horns
oh yes I took the bull by the horns
I put a hammerlock on the steering wheel
and a forged note from the City of Victoria
license suspended
did it in the dead of night
didn't sleep a wink
I watched tv all night long
wondering when my father would discover it
my little conspiracy
behold my own son seeks my car
all night long I watched the Olympics from Nagano
I watched Elvis skate with a pulled groin muscle
win a silver in a wrenching howl of pain
he never even blinked till he was done
my dad had gotten through to Elvis
if it hurts don't let it show
all his life behind the wheel my dad
had been free as a rustler
I had just shot his horse
you want to sleep at night guys
don't shoot your father's horse

a few years ago
he told me his secret
after the heart attack I said
I just want to make it to seventy
I hit seventy and I said well seventy-five
when I made it to seventy-five
and your mother and I moved out here
all my arteries were shot
but the little ones the
capillaries
yeah   the capillaries
they took up the job
so I said wouldn't it be great
if I made it all the way to eighty
and I made it to eighty
well   I'll never make it to ninety
any fool knows I'll never make it to ninety
so why not shoot for eighty-five   eh

my father will be ninety-four this summer
because the capillaries took up the job
the century will expire before my father does
this country will expire before my father does

on the subject of death
don't get involved

how did you get out here
I drove
how
I said I drove
in that car of yours

he wanders at night
sometimes into the wrong apartment
the people who run the building want to kick him out
send Mum and Dad to a nursing home
lie around with a bunch of old duffers
no thanks he says
no thanks my mother says
they'll have to drag us out in a box he says
can we change the subject my mother says
how did you get out here

I flew out one time to say goodbye
he had gone outside to check on his car
gone out in the dark in his nightshirt
lost his balance and grabbed for the rail
the rail turned out to be a vine and he crashed
into a pile of cinder blocks
broke five ribs and collapsed a lung
crawled inside   gasping
Mum phoned the ambulance
(never let your guard down)
I arrived at the ICU
as soon as Mum saw me she shook her head
the gesture meant no
he's not going to make it
the oxygen they pumped into him had gone astray
Instead of the usual scrawny carcass
I beheld my father puffed up like the pillsbury doughboy
subcutaneous emphysema
he recognized me
had a dream   makes me feel like a fool
some guy was after me   in an alley
couldn't see him very well   looked like a thug
he knew I was hurt   couldn't move or fight back

so I played possum   pulled in my leg
when he came up on me   shoot me or something
stab me   I kicked out with my leg
woke up   I'd knocked over the bedside table
the bedpan   felt like a fool
that was Death   I said
and he wheezed with laughter
the next day he complained about cold soup
the day after that he tyrannized the nurses
the day after that he declared war on the ICU
tore a strip off his loving wife
tore another strip off me
my dad was on the mend

the millennium will expire
before my father dies
cancer heart stroke dementia aphasia
alzheimer's collapsed lungs
Death stalking him down a dark alley

never let your guard down Death
or my dad will kick you in the nuts

this was meant to be a song
the song of David for Saul
really   it should be a song
Dave to Saul
rhymes and all

in the meantime he has
his food brought to him
regular transfusions of rye
his disabled car
his wife and sons
their worried looks
their wary love

(1999)

North of Here

Four hundred miles north of Edmonton
but the stream was warm enough
and he young enough to wade
in short pants and runners
opaque slow rusty water
some shallow holes
no fish biting

He could hear the humming of yellowjackets
in the jackpine among rumoured bears
hear chipping sparrows and shrikes
call the name of the river
Christina Christina

Then he found a hole so fishy he almost staked a claim
the stream flowing between two flat boulders
forming a pool big enough to hold anything
you could ever imagine

He cast his spoon and let it sink until it disappeared
bumping along the sandy bottom
     nothing
          nothing
               nothing
so he waded out
up to his armpits
in water dark as whisky
made it out to the boulders
when something much too big
slid between his legs

Didn't remember jumping
he just shot up out of the water
onto the rock like a bucked rider
looked down into the amber current
still clutching his rod in a shaky hand
knowing that it lived down there and he did not

Because he was young
he hooked the great fish
dragged it spiralling up from its lair
and because he was young
he bludgeoned the great fish
long green and perfect longer than his leg
until it stopped thrashing
hung it by the gills in a tree
had his lunch by the stream
thinking wasn't he the lad
wasn't he the lad

When he returned hungry in the late afternoon
the fish was still hanging there
covered with yellowjackets
feasting fat on the meat
the gaping pike jaws
humming their beesong
the yellowjackets flew away
engorged like drunkards bounced
off each other and branches of trees
easy pickings for shrikes and sparrows

The next morning his fish was gone
all but a few strips of skin
a length of spine
the fish's body
it was everywhere now
off humming off warbling in the trees
grunting in the dark thickets of the nearby scrub
from fish to flesh to scat
all but tatters of skin

He picked up a piece of skin
taken by the green of it
dark scales flecked with gold
like chain mail

Up north he learned the usual things
that nothing is wasted
everything eats and shits
everything gets eaten and shat
but up north he also learned
that men walk in water
fish hang in trees
bees birds and bears
assemble like a well-fed choir
and sing the song of the pike

(2000)

Goddamned Boat

Not the elephants.
They were always too grand.

Tigers? Thumbs down.
Too fierce, too beautiful.
Might get ideas if allowed to roam.

Lions? Ditto.
They don't have the proper humility.
They don't fear us.

Leopards?
Exterminate the brutes.
Especially snow leopards.
Gone. Fuck em.

Cheetahs, then.
Okay, but only on leashes
for photo ops.

Hyenas? Yes. Of course.
Let there be hyenas.
Not too proud to feed on corpses.

Songbirds. (Oh, God. Why me?
Why do I always have to be Mr. Meany?)
Well, that's a problem isn't it.
Songbirds are a problem, yer damn right.
Annoying habits.
They eat insects that farmers and gardeners have sprayed.
They die and it looks pathetic.
And who gets shit for that?
Not the songbirds.
They sing too early in the morning.
If allowed to come aboard
they could drown out my new sound system.
With all those larks or canaries or whatever
squawking all the time
We couldn't even listen to CNN.
Nyet to songbirds.

Cockroaches? Yes.
They've got the genes to survive in a global economy.
Let there be cockroaches.

Rats? I suppose so.
Impossible to kill.
Not even junk food can kill a rat.
If you can't beat em, join em.

Eagles? No.
Their feathers are worth a fortune.
Makes more sense to harvest eagles.
But buzzards, yeah, let there be buzzards.
They're already thick as mosquitoes these days.
I don't care. I do not care.
You deaf or somethin?
I said, let there be buzzards.
Remember, this is my goddam boat.

(2000)

His Last Poem

or

The Future of Guy Poetry in Western Canada

for Guy Gunckel

This here's my last poem
that's right   you heard me
it's the end of the line
I'm tired of all the bullshit
what do you mean *what bullshit*
do I have to spell it out for you
okay you're a good listener
so I'll tell you
maybe it's just a guy thing   okay
but I'm tired of knocking myself out
and then having some neophyte with a nazi haircut
who calls himself an editor
carve up my work for dinner

I'm tired of jerkoff critics
reading things into my poems
and those myopic slugs who
read for literary magazines
and sit on your work for nineteen months
and don't even offer you the courtesy of a rejection note
and I'm tired of reading for a roomful of potatoes
who nod politely at your readings and then
slink out of the room for fear of contamination
I'm tired of the late nights and smoky

hey
don't fall asleep on me
I mean if I'm *boring you* I'll stop
but don't forget   you're the one who asked
where was I   oh yeah
I'm tired of all the bullshit
I'm tired of all those groupies that wait for you
when you enter the lecture halls
the women who sidle up to you with beckoning eyes
of course they do
you never been to a reading
well then   there you go
like a pack of panthers   no guff
but they don't want you for the obvious reasons
no sirree
they want to lure you back home
to read their goddam poems
so I'm quitting
I don't care how much people beg me
fuck the public
they can whine all they want
this cowboy's gonna hang up his spurs
I'm outa here

this will be my last book of poems
this thing I'm working on
this will be my last poem
they can beg me all they want
I can't stand it when they beg me
makes me feel like Dylan or someone
I have to go on with my life
I've got things to do   places to go
hell   this   right here
this might be my very last line
my very last line of poetry

except   you know what
they won't let me quit
I'm like this old sheriff
he wants to hang up his gun
but there's some bad outlaws coming
and the people
well   you know the story
no?
maybe it's a guy thing
I mean I'm tired of the expectations
you know what I mean
the expectations   yeah
you walk into a room full of people
and what they're thinking is
oh there's the famous poet
I wonder what he's thinking
let the bard speak eh
and what if
just what if
on that particular day
I don't feel like saying anything profound

what if I just want to talk about
the goddam right rear tire on my car
it's already been plugged four times
and now it has this pinhole leak
and I takes it in and the dufus behind the counter
he says *Sir I think it's a new tire you need*
what if that's all I wanted to talk about
I mean you can't be profound all the time
you can't spend every waking hour
worried about existential dilemmas
or the way your space-time continuum gets warped all to shit
I mean even a poet wants the chance to
be a regular guy now and then

Well that's it for me
no more collections of my work
no more pictures of my mug in the bookstore window
I'm outa here
this is my last poem
this is my last line
this is the last word
I've always wanted to get in the last word
Well there it is
Adios amigos
so long
what
a pizza?
you wanna go out for pizza at this hour?
hell no   let's phone for one from my room
Yeah   let's get acquainted
see what I'm sayin?

Oh yeah
one more thing
you're not a poet are you
oh   nothin
just wondered
let's go

(2001)

The Naming of March

in March the puddles melt the
puddles freeze the puddles
melt the puddles freeze
she loves me
she loves me not
depends which day you ask her
March lasts about a year and a half
like the last eighteen months
before puberty

unlike the verb
that bristles with determination
there is no determination in March
no spring in its stride
don't be fooled by the arch in March
there is no arch in March

March: after the war god Mars
who commands the storms
spits out flashes of lightning
naming March after the war god
is liked naming our cat
after the Goddess of Wisdom
in March the cat comes
in the cat goes out

People of Saskatoon
we need a new name for March
Flossy or Floyd or perhaps
the name of my nextdoor neighbour
Merton Waffel

March is a field with ragged patches of snow
an endless feast of nothing
in a restaurant with no specialty
we serve whatever's goin
little bit a those
little bit a these
little bit a melt
little bit a freeze

the light returns
the spring equinox
on someone else's door
straggles of barking geese
circle the fields
they know something I don't
that winter will lose this round
then again   maybe not

(2001)

At Night, the Writers

for all the writers on retreat at St. Peter's Abbey, Muenster, Saskatchewan

It's after midnight in the kitchen
thirty-one below and the popcorn's all gone
the sink is full of wineglasses and mugs
writers are slumped around the table
like a bunch of old shoes
all worn out but the tongues
words are getting harder to come by
like the sound of a tommy gun
laughter erupts in staccato bursts
the conversation rolls over
silence threatens
dread silence

One by one the words are slipping off to bed
the writers watch them go
now they're leaving in groups
the nouns detach themselves from the verbs
mumble their way out the kitchen door
mutter down the dark hallway
reluctantly the modifiers follow
expletives still want to party
they and the indefinite articles
will be the last to go
and then the writers

All through the winter night
in a storm of letters
they flounder after lost words
letters stick to their brains like fridge magnets
no no no you don't understand
it's words I'm looking for
the writers in pajamas
standing beneath the windows
of their favourite lost words
holler *Stel la!   Stella-a-a-a!*

Morning comes too soon
I wake to the clang of cathedral bells
dislodge from my teeth
just the husk
of a kernel of corn

(2001)

89

Mum Puts on Her Lipstick

Ninety-one   almost blind
she refuses to go to supper without lipstick
It covers a multitude of sins she tells me

In a gnarled hand she holds the mirror
wedding present from the Great Depression
holds the tube in the other

At first there is no contact
the lips extrude and tremble
her lipstick flutters and bobs in space

approaches with a bee's logic
bright missile homing
on a blind target

I have become a participant
open my own mouth and lean forward just like her
the lipstick feints to the left   jerks back

She seems to catch a glimpse of her face
I look like the wreck of the Hesperus
and there is contact

Her hand shakes
the mirror shakes
the lipstick hovers at her mouth

but it's found the mark
does its poppy work
her lips glide together till the job is done

Ye gods, stand up for old women
praise for their everlasting vanity
praise for the lipstick that lights on beauty in the dark

(2001)

Two Poems for July

Then came Hot July boyling like to fire,
That all his garments he had cast away.

Edmund Spenser, "The Faerie Queen"

1. Killdeer

Between here and town
the farms drift and wilt
under blasts of hot wind.
No more shorebirds
no more ducks
no more muskrats
the only wildlife
a roadkill fawn in the ditch.
This is the end of hope.
This is the end of the world.

During lunch in a small café
you hear the wind whimpering to get in
then howling like a coyote bitch
supplications to the god
of scattered things.

Later from a nearby slough
this whole scene cries out
right from the source of it all,
a calling bird with grit and alkali
and high weeping in the voice.
Today this mother of all winds
has whelped a killdeer.

(1998)

2. The End of the Drought

One dark cloud has commandeered
the western Horizon
moves like Fate over the parched city
a crackling bruiseblue eminence
smelling of rain

Der Blitz schlägt ein—the signature
of God scribbled across the sky
Hot July with a pool cue
black ball cracks to the corner pocket
rumbles all the way down under

Like go-go dancers on the last day
the aspens toss and whip and lean one way
and the rain comes
it comes down
like a dream of Atlantis

(2002)

Call Waiting

for Kever

My agent won't return my calls   her way of reminding me
that she lives in Toronto   and I do not   my publisher doesn't phone me
just sits on my manuscript in order to look down
on writers from greater heights   and this is the one that will put me
over the top   this one glows in the dark

Salman Rushdie never phones me   think of the
conversations we could have
    Bummer about the fatwa   I would say
    Yes Carpenter as you say a bummer
    He might ask me if the Riders have a chance this year
    You never know Salman stranger things have happened

Politicians and businessmen   people with power in my province
they're all excited about building yet another dam on the Saskatchewan
I could tell them it's a dumb idea   just another IUD in the womb of the
nation   but do they phone me for advice and wisdom

No one phones me   that's how they define themelves   by not phoning
me   they meet for coffee to recount the many times
they have forgone the privilege   old friends who used to call me up
don't call anymore   my own mother no longer phones me   she's too old
to use the phone   I'd settle for a call that begins
   Hello Sir and how are you this evening

But yesterday morning you phoned me   something about your shift at
the library   and would I hold supper   something about walking to
work over the bridge in the falling snow   a note you strike like a phone
when at last it rings   that then I scorn to change my state with kings

(2002)

How do you know you're going to fly?

A basement room at the monastery, cluttered and cold like a root cellar, a place where strangers are not welcome. I am looking at statues of saints and virgins, dust and cobwebs. Light from a dirty window.

Magic is in the room. It hovers around the bust of Saint Polycarp, a bishop in Smyrna. The old martyr is coming to life. He gets his legs back, smiles like a man long dead, swims past me and into the brick wall, turns to do another lap. A voice whispers do not speak his name!

When I speak his name his gargoyle head is worming out of the mortar. He stiffens, cast in the bronze of a half-formed grimace. His magic flows into me, palpable as dust and cobwebs. I am going to fly.

How do you know you're going to fly before your feet leave the floor? You just know. The act of letting go requires no faith, no prayer for safety, no final inhalation before you take off. You do it because it is in you. Like a blow-up doll of myself, heart bursting with helium, I float up the steps to the light and warmth of the cathedral.

I get looks from the monks singing psalms in the chapel. *Now what is he up to? Oh God, not the flying martyr thing. Brother Basil must have left the door open again.* There are better things to do than gawk at a floating poet. The monks get on with their psalms. This is a good moment. I decide not to resent their indifference.

(2002)

A Few Words for January

I

Say you are leaving a 12th-floor lounge
where people have been watching other
people on a giant screen
the televised ones are from
New York Melbourne London Rio Melbourne again
dancing countdowns streamers madness
maxed-out merriment in every frame
Say you descend by the elevator
next to an embracing couple
out you go into the wind without your gloves
a wind that freezes your forehead till it aches
opens razor burns on your face
you find your car unplugged
let's say in the excitement of the approaching
millennium you just forgot
of course your car won't start
you look up at the glittering night
feel the exhalations of the polar wind
the tinkle of icicles dropping onto your windshield

your fingers
where are your fingers
they feel like aching stumps
and is it the Apocalypse then
the end of all you know and love

No
just the beginning
just January
spitting out the bones of December.
So what you do is
you head back into the hotel
trying to remember the remedy for frostbite
glasses fogged
looking for a doorman
an elevator
a friend
a cigarette
a cup of kindness.

2

Beginnings are difficult
life before beginnings was probably easier
if only you could remember
but January waits for no one
hangovers be damned
the new year must be born and you with it

you ease yourself out of bed
feet touch floor
toes vulnerable
before you can get dressed you must
remove your pajamas
cowering will not be tolerated

month of Janus
guardian of portals and beginnings
he likes to look back to the good old days and
forward to warmer times
it's *now* that's always the problem

now as you walk
down the shovelled path to the car
wrapped in woolen garments once extolled by grandparents
your boots begin to squeak like dying rodents
there is some old-fashioned courage in this moment
like deciding to go off life-support

stooped before the long cord
poking out from the grille of your car
you are a fetus gasping its first astonished breath
yank out the cord

(2002)

heart like a frog

his love asleep // the air green and humming // around her
boggy fresh and // when she smiles from waking // purlings &
warblings // from the redwing blackbirds of his heart // like a
frog he loves to cling // to the lily pads of her breasts // sleeping
or waking her muskeg mass // is the *schaumgummi* of love // so
like a marsh is she // where gadwalls gabble quackhappy in her
waters // ribbet the limbs ribbet the breast // ribbet the nose
her ears her toes // a ribbet apiece to all the rest // that ebbs
and flows in sweet repose // and don't forget the other breast //
and if a frog defines his essence // then let him drown in her
tumescence // the alarm

The alarm clock has done its work.
He wades from bed to bathroom.
Bedroom flippers flap on the floor
head of cattail
aloft between his legs.
At last he pours the coffee and
Flippers? Did he say flippers?
He looks down at his feet.
Surely they are called slippers.

(2002)

Tent Caterpillars

for Doug and Barb

They climb the trunks to
reach the branches and leaves
their probing bodies soft like the
fingers of uninvited lovers
enough bluestriped larvae
to make the valley crawl

In the silences
between the trillings of songbirds
we hear the worms masticate the leaves
in the writhing branches hear them
discharge their faeces
tiny black pellets
pelting down on the duff below
ravines and bluffs
pastures and gullies
everything green fades to grey

At last the sated worms
roll into their tents
wrap themselves in silk
the leaves curl up around them
turn brown and die

Four hundred square miles of
denuded trees
dreaming worms in cotton candy
a new kind of urban sprawl
kneedeep in silk we wade
like shorebirds after an oilspill

Before long the moths rise in
brown waves from their cocoons
(count them in millions)
the breeding has begun
the females work their magic on stems and twigs
bands of eggs like caviar
(count them in billions)

Next spring the worms will return
like Greed and Gluttony at a morality play
like eager shoppers
like smiling land speculators
like summer cottagers
like tv children at the breakfast table
like slow street gangs
like the great hominids swarming the earth
who named the worms

(2002)

Notes on My Mother, Marjorie Carpenter (1910—2002)

I

She loved to dance, tell jokes, read, but singing was at the top of the list. In the kitchen she was always humming tunes that her man and two boys could only croak. Once in a while, without embarrassment or apology, she would belt out a fullthroated song that made you pay attention. *Blue skies smilin at me nothin but cruising down the river on a Sunday afternoon, the one you love they call her Frivolous Sal, a peculiar sort of a gal I hate to see* (my favourite) *that evening sun go down folks out walkin pitchin woo here am I here is you oh do do do something they call her Hardhearted Hanna the vamp of Savanna meanest gal in town.* For the sentimental ones she had a high clear tremolo, for the funny ones a nasal twang. She kept time with foot and fist and if you sang along you had to keep the beat and stay on key. Singing was serious.

2

I am six years old. My friends and I (Watson, Wilmot, Elliott and brother Pete) have found a young bird that must have tumbled from a nest in our lane. A thrush or a robin would be my guess. We bring it up the lane to my mother, present it to her like an award. She holds the bird in one hand, shields and strokes it with the other. I remember a certain expression on her face that I will not attempt to describe. Well into middle age I came across a black and white photo of my mother holding the nestling and yes, the same expression on her face, one of those rare moments when an old memory survives a million opportunities for distortion. The beak is open, the bird tilts its head up to her face, we are gathered around her gawking at the downy miracle in her hand. All mouths open. The more I look at the picture the more I see that the subjects in the snapshot are less engaging than the thing they are all caught up in. Five children, a mother, a bird, but what you notice is the watching. Is the bird waiting for a worm? Imprinting on my mother? Are we five imprinting on the bird?

3

I'm in my twenties. Dad and Mr. Massie, his son Bruce, brother Pete and I have been driving the sideroads in a futile search for grouse, listening to the World Series on the radio. It is Thanksgiving Monday and it's been raining for hours. My mother and Mrs. Massie spend the day preparing the big dinner. They hear a thump against the cottage window. My mother goes outside to investigate. Birdless, the men come home to the consolations of scotch, roast turkey, and a late addition to the meal, a roasted grouse with not one pellet in the flesh.

4

I'm in my thirties, doing the annual visit with Mum and Dad. My mother wears a bright orange blouse in the house at Paul's Terrace. We gather for drinks on the veranda and all at once the hummingbirds arrive, several of them. They take turns buzzing around her shoulders, perhaps intent on trying out a massive new flower. They are anything but gentle with one another. Nestlings, budgies, dead birds, exotics, they flock around my memories of her. With Dad it was always pool tables, golf, hunting, fish in the creel, cars and gadgets. With Mum it's always birds and singing, singing and birds. For a few years she was a hobby painter and all she ever did was mallards.

5

Five days after her final stroke, after a long night of apnea, death rattles and morphine, she died just short of ninety-two. My wife and I came home and slept through the day and I woke up in a state of predictable numbness and a sound I had never heard before. It began with bright tinkling notes on a descending scale, whistled notes and warbled phrases that rose in pitch like small bubbles through an ocarina, the sort of trilling that could only come from a land where orchids and mangos were commonplace. The bird was perched in our plum tree, slightly smaller than a robin, a brilliant orange warbler nowhere to be found in any of our books. It stayed for three days, sang tirelessly morning and evening, then flew away.

6

There's a poem in here somewhere. I only have to remember the nestling in my mother's hand, the way she stroked it with a finger, and I must admit: I'm tempted to do something with this. Maybe some other day. Or maybe this is the poem for my mother that never gets written. At the moment I'm thinking of these notes as a gathering of twigs and grass from which something irretrievable has fallen to earth.

(2002)

Acknowledgements

A number of these poems have appeared previously in the following places: *Dandelion, Grain, Briar Patch,* several Coteau Books anthologies, *Cross-Canada Writers' Quarterly, Fiddlehead, Kaleidescope,* and *Paris/Atlantic.* Several poems have been broadcast nationally on CBC radio programs, *Morningside, Basic Black,* and *Sounds Like Canada,* and several others on CBC Saskatchewan's *Ambience* and *Gallery,* and shown on SCN's *Literary Moment* series. Many thanks to the people behind these public spaces where poetry can be read and heard.

For nearly three decades in Saskatoon, many good poets, too many to mention, have tried to prepare me for the rigours of writing poetry. We have met at Anne Szumigalski's house, the Kerrs' house, Elizabeth Brewster's apartment, the Brennas' acreage, Smitty's living room, and read to each other on many retreats throughout Saskatchewan. Thanks go to the Coteau board members, especially Geoffrey Ursell, who took a chance on a card-carrying prose writer; thanks to Bill Robertson, Lorna Crozier, and Don Kerr; special thanks go to Dave Margoshes and to Kever, who had to read all of these pieces in early drafts; and to Don McKay for his thoughtful, constructive, and witty guidance.

About the Author

David Carpenter has been working on and off at the poems that appear in *Trout Stream Creed,* his first poetry collection, since 1964. During that time he has written seven other books, including the novel *Banjo Lessons,* published by Coteau in 1997, which won the City of Edmonton Book Prize. He has appeared in literary festivals all across the country and had his poems broadcast a number of times on television and national radio. Carpenter was born in Edmonton of Saskatchewan parents and moved to Saskatoon to teach in 1975. He continues to live in Saskatoon, where he writes full-time.